The Candy Maker Resume
Resume Writing Hacks

Resume Psychology Series

Dirk Spencer

The Candy Maker Resume
Resume Writing Hacks

Table of Contents

Introduction

The Candy Maker Resume – Resume Writing Hacks is for people who want a detailed, step-by-step, how-to example of researching and creating relevant and compelling resume content in an efficient and repeatable manner.

Since we learn best when we help others we need an imaginary job-seeker: Sara Elf. She is a Candy Maker.

You, the reader, will be the recruiter trying to place Sara with a prominent candy company. The problem here is two-fold: Sara's resume is horrible, and you have no experience with candy other than eating it.

This book is based on my lecture series by the same name with all of my notes and explanations.

There will also be a before-and-after version of Sara's resume for comparison. There will also be a debrief on Sara's "after" resume.

In the end, you should be able to generate resume content for yourself with confidence in a systematic and expedient fashion. This will allow you to rapidly customize your content for each job submission, which should improve your chances of being interviewed.

My Bias Against Examples

One of the pet peeves of recruiters and hiring managers is the use of resume templates. Why?

- They were poorly formatted
- Wasted a lot of real estate with empty white-space
- Used tables to control content

During my lectures, people would ask for a template of my suggested resume layout.

I did not have one.

I did not want to create one.

Why?

My bias against resume templates or examples is based on some crude assumptions about what people needed to be:

- Able to write their own resume content
- Skilled in using word processor commands
- Knowledgeable using word processor formatting commands

Plus, I was confident the processes outlined in *Resume Psychology* (RP) were simple enough for anyone to master. In my pea-sized brain, I was sure business professionals seeking employment would:

- Rise to the occasion and figure it out
- Ask for help if they needed it

It seemed reasonable. They had a 60 to 90-minute live lecture and a 20-page handout to take home. Samples were reviewed, marked-up and returned to their owner with a tip-sheet listing many of the things they should do.

My friends Blane and Larry had other ideas.

My Brothers from Other Mothers

I have these friends named "Blane" and "Larry."

These men have been friends for some time in the truest sense of the word.

It is their continued support and nudging which forced me to re-think how I taught *Resume Psychology* (RP).

Blane was very direct and to the point. Blane understood my concerns about having an example available. But he was first on the scene suggesting and requesting an example of how-to create resume content for people who did not understand the lecture or the handouts.

Then there was Larry. He attended several of my lectures and was always supportive of the methods. What I did not know he was he was not so clear on my *brilliance*, either. Like Blane, he said people needed examples of "how to" do *Resume Psychology* (RP).

In the end, I finally created a how-to example. It was created on the fly during a series of emails and phone calls with someone who was desperate for a generic how-to walk-thru process or other rubric to mimic.

To this day, I give Blane credit for planting the seeds and cultivating the idea over the long-haul. He was a friend even when I was not interested in creating this content.

Larry gets credit for harvesting the crop. His urging for providing an example forced me to create the Candy Maker lecture.

The Candy Maker

The Candy Maker lecture was born out of a real-time improvisation.

The lecture started with a rip-off of the "Got Milk?" campaign. At the time it seemed clever enough.

Got Resume Content?

This is where the PowerPoint slide would project the resume of Sara Elf. Her resume was deliberately:

- Brief
- Simple
- Vague

The goal was to show an exaggeration of an empty or incomplete resume.

The idea was to show people a process for developing resume content under these extreme conditions:

- No experience with the job function
- No reference point within the resume
- No experience with the industry associated with the job

In the end people would understand how they could adapt these strategies (i.e. method) to their needs with confidence.

In the end, you should be able to:

- Be more effective in researching keywords
- Develop relevant resume content quickly
- Have a high degree of confidence about your resume
- Be able to re-engineer or re-express experiences
- Present the same experiences from multiple points of view

The Candy Maker – Sara Elf

Poof! You are now a recruiter.

You received a job order (job opening) from your client, our imaginary confectionary company. They need a full-time candy maker.

Your job assignment is simple: source, screen and hire a candy-maker.

Being good friends you call me (the author) and shares your good news of becoming a recruiter and having your first job order.

However, your luck has run out, as you can only find one candy maker and her resume is horrible. You need help "beefing out the resume" and call me for assistance.

But before you can actually get my help, I laugh loudly into the phone receiver and say something obnoxious, like: "I hope it is not Sara Elf. She must have the worst resume in the history of candy-makers."

The last thing you hear before the "click" is me laughing hysterically.

This means *you* have to fix the resume on your own.

Elf Resumes Suck

Below is your candy maker's resume:

Sara Elf
Candy Maker
NotElfingAround@Gmail.Com

Professional Experience

Candy Master, Inc.   February 2000 to Present
Candy Maker   Elf Village, NP
- Make Candy
- Sell Candy

Masters of Candy, LLC   March 1995 to May 2000
Candy Maker   Elf-in Way, NP
- Make Candy
- Sell Candy

Candies R Us   January 1881 to May 1995
Candy Maker   Clause Town, NP
- Make Candy
- Sell Candy

Impressed? She made candy. She sold candy. That is it. Two

lines, two words each. You have to fix this.

Candy Made – Candy Sold

As you can see Sara's resume is a whole lot of nothing.

She *made* candy. She *sold* candy. We have no further

information. Yes, this is an exaggeratedly vague example but

there are people who create similarly vague resumes. Vague

resume content is likely the reason most people do not receive

calls for jobs!

Candy Maker Resume Review

Some of Sara's resume issues include:

- Lack of a phone number
- Email name is on the salacious side
- Use of non-numerical months for job-dates
- Number of jobs listed based on the tenure

The Good News

Sara does have a solid resume layout. She is using a reverse chronological format. The reverse chronological format is important because:

- It is what hiring managers are expecting
- It is the format used in applicant tracking systems

These application tracking or resume databases have different names as each vendor is selling to a target audience. Some of the generic labels include:

- Resume Database (or Resume Tracker)
- Applicant Tracking Software (ATS)
- Applicant Tracking System (ATS)
- Customer Relationship Management (CRM)
- Vendor Management Software (VMS)

These products come in different price points. They can be complex to simple. Either way, they impact your resume each and every time.

Save Sara's Resume

How do we save Sara's resume? What would we research? Where could we research? How fast could we do this work?

Start Simple

Perhaps the easiest place to start is to ask ourselves simple

and obvious questions like these:

- What kind of candy did she make?
- How was the candy made?
- How was the candy sold?
- Where did she sell it?
- Where did she make it?
- How much candy are we talking about?

The downside to developing our own questions is a lack of:

- Expertise in the candy making industry
- Knowledge of best practices, processes or regulations
- Determining what content is most relevant to the market

Learning and Applying Techniques

We need to do a few things at the same time with resume

content:

- Develop specifics by each skill or experience
- Transcend vague content to create details
- Transcend detailed content to create granular specifics
- We want to ensure the granularity is relevant
- We want techniques which produce content quickly

To do this we can do research and attack the material

systematically.

What we practice on Sara's resume can be used on your

resume. Sometimes helping someone else is the best way to

master a new skill.

Step #1: Construct the Work-Vocabulary

Maybe it would be more accurate to say re-construct or reconnect to your work-related vocabulary?

To do this is simple, we do word association. Nothing complicated or sexy.

We interrogate our existing vocabulary to develop more content. This will lead to more choices in describing the work experience.

Step 2: Make Lists!

Instead of trying to remember it all in our short-term memory we need to make a list. This reduces mental stress while creating content.

Step 3: Identify Current Keywords

We start our word association exercise with the words we already have. Sara's keywords included:

- "Candy"
- "Made"
- "Sold"

By using the word associations and lists we can generate content quickly with confidence.

Step 4: Assess Resume Granularity

In Sara's resume there is no granularity. Her resume would be the complete opposite of granular content.

The word candy by its definition is vague and broad. It lacks specificity.

Step 5: Managing Resume Granularity

Ask yourself, what is the current level of granularity in the resume.

In Sara's case the answer is zero so any increase in granularity will make it a better resume. We need a context to shape the 3-words we have (i.e. Candy, Made, Sold) without turning her resume into a recipe book.

Which brings about the question: What level of granularity works best for the typical resume?

The answer depends on three things:

- What is missing on the resume
- What the job requires
- Your level of effort

What is missing on the Resume?

People tend to favor one style of content over another when creating their resume.

The risks of too much or too little specificity is significant.

People are turned off by extremes in style.

Too little and people are unable to form an image of you as having enough skills.

Too much detail and people zone-out because their short-term memory is overloaded.

What are the Job Requirements?

Answers to this question can be tricky. People get wrapped up in what the job description states. The bad news about job descriptions is they are typically pieced together from multiple sources which probably do not effectively represent the work to be done.

This means people need to be engaged in their industry and peers to "know" what the job should be and align their resume accordingly.

To do this effectively know the relative differences among the following generic job concepts:

- Nuances across business units
- Old-school standards yet replaced
- New-school trends yet adopted
- Trends with certifying bodies
- Association and guild related politics
- Regulatory or legislative changes
- Bestselling authors across all media

- Conference speakers past and present

It is a lot to know but it is critical to fashioning your experience in multiple contexts or multiple points of view. The ability to take a solitary slice of an experience and showcase it from multiple perspectives is the objective.

This creates redundancy giving you more options to customize the resume for each job opening.

This is how the professionals differentiate their "expertise" from the amateurs with "experience."

Being able to compare and contrast information in your industry is key to being an expert.

Being able to delineate the anthropology of your work experience against what happened in your industry will cause you to present better content. Being able to explain the evolution of terminology and practice over a multi-year period proves your expertise and telegraphs your passion.

Your level of Effort?

Like everything else in life you reap what you sow. The same is true for resume content. Be willing to drill down and do the work.

In Sara's case we are going to do the heavy lifting in order to master the process for our own resume.

List Making 101 – Word Association

Unpacking the word candy! What words come to mind when you say the word "candy"?

During my lectures, the audience will deliver two very broad categories:

- Hard
- Soft

Would discussing the differences between hard candy and soft candy improve the granularity of Sara's resume?

Absolutely!

With hard and soft candy, we start our list. This will show variety and help create granular content. It might look something like this:

Hard and Soft Candy Varieties

- Mints
- Suckers
- Gums
- Licorice
- Jelly beans
- Jaw Breakers
- Fish

If we follow this idea of granularity or specificity, we might come up with another list.

What Kind of Candy?

- Lemon Drops
- Chocolate Bars
- Fudge Bark
- Candied Nuts
- Chocolate Covered Fruit –
- Marsh Mello Chicks
- Holiday Candy

Deconstructing Kinds of Candy

From the previous list we can compare items to drive home the idea of granularity by asking a few questions to know if we have the best details at our disposal.

Lemon Drops

Are lemon drops specific enough?

Do they clearly define the type of candy?

What synonyms can we use to create more accurate or more specific data about our skills with lemon drops?

Some ideas to consider for the word "lemon":

- Sour
- Tart

Ideas for the word "drop:"

- Sucker
- Pop
- Chewable

This nets us additional candy types we might use instead of

lemon drop, such as:

- Sour Sucker
- Sour Pop
- Tart Chews

Chocolate Bars

When you read "chocolate" did your mind race to specifics

similar to any of these different types of chocolate?

- Dark Chocolate
- Milk Chocolate
- Sweet Chocolate
- Semisweet Chocolate
- Bittersweet Chocolate
- White Chocolate

With this detail we can create more compelling content about

Sara's chocolate bar experience. This would be most useful

when applying to companies which specialize in one of the

options on the list.

Candied Nuts

I omitted fudge bark because, well, I could not develop

alternative names for it. If you can, great. If not, well, then fudge

bark might be specific enough.

But nuts would be easy, right? When you read "candied nuts" do you visualize your preferred edible kernel? Technically nuts are a form of fruit. But the most obvious detail to substitute for "nut" would be the specific type of nut used. That list might include:

- Coconuts
- Peanuts
- Almonds
- Cashews
- Macadamias
- Chestnuts
- Hazelnuts
- Pecans
- Pistachios
- Walnuts
- Salted Nuts
- Seasoned Nuts
- Roasted Nuts
- Macadamia

Candied coconut or candied almonds provide a clearer picture of Sara's skills which is more accurate. This would be helpful where a company specialized in one of these product offerings. This is the value of drilling down on words over and over again until we hit the most accurate or clear representation.

Having more options will nearly always net better content for the resume.

Chocolate Covered Fruit

We did chocolate once and could re-use that list here and potentially have enough detail.

But like with "candied nuts" do you see or maybe smell your preferred fruit reading "chocolate covered fruit"?

Again to achieve granularity we would develop a list of fruit based on experience:

- Fresh
- Dried
- Strawberries
- Cherries
- Raspberries
- Pineapple
- Apple
- Banana

It might be one kind. In that case, "Chocolate Covered Fruit" might sound more experienced when compared to "Chocolate Covered Apples" (i.e. oranges, pineapples, strawberries).

What about synonyms for the word "Covered"? Could we use words like *dipped* or *drizzled* to showcase a chocolatier's sophistication? Is this process making sense? Can you do this for your resume? You bet!

Marsh Mellow Chicks

Ditto ala fudge bark for marsh mellow chicks. Is that granular enough? Maybe? There are marsh mellow rabbits, flowers and hearts? Maybe we need to think smarter here. What about things like:

- Flavor combinations
- Holiday themes
- Color options

It is easy to slack off with this being an artificial example, right? I get it. It feels silly.

But would these versions beat out the original example given:

- Vanilla Flavored Marsh Mellow Chicks
- Easter Marsh Mellow Chicks
- Dyed Marsh Mellow Chicks

Would "Dyed Multi-Color Easter Marsh Mellow Chicks" be over-kill? Maybe. *The goal is to teach yourself how to deconstruct each experience to create better content and exercise judgement about which content best represents the experience.*

Holiday Candy

Hopefully when you saw the word "Holiday Candy" your mind raced to Hanukkah or Christmas or Halloween. The list could be rather long which allows for more options based on each situation.

Could we use the word "seasonal" candy during the interview to change it up a bit? Sure!

Would "Seasonal Holiday Easter Candy" be over-kill? Again, we would want to create a list to leverage the brain-storming activity and evaluate options later. Our list could be this straight forward:

- Valentines
- Christmas
- Easter
- Rocha Hashanah
- Halloween
- Decorative Candy (parties, weddings, anniversaries)

Decorative Candy

Our list for decorative candy could be very traditional:

- Foil Wrapped
- Velvet Boxes
- Baskets and Bows
- Bags and Ribbons
- Hearts Shaped Containers
- Egg Shaped containers
- Tree Ornaments

Unpacking "Made"

We can uncork the word "made" with:

- Mix
- Process

Concepts that go with mixed and processed include:

- Combine
- Swirl
- Separate
- Pack
- Cook
- Pour
- Liquefy
- Chemical reaction
- Pulling
- Stretching

Unpacking "Made" Tools of the Trade

Mentioning specific tools may not be super exciting, but it would

add another layer of context. It could be the piece of information

missing from a competitor resume! Things like:

- Spoons
- Forks
- Spatulas
- Copper bowls
- Electric mixers
- Wall hooks
- Candy rollers
- Candy wrappers
- Marble Tops
- Rolling Pins

Unpacking "Made" Ingredients

More texture can be had with details thought to be too obvious

when making candy. But the devil is in the details so

ingredients should be mentioned:

- Sugar
- Spice
- Flour
- Flavoring
- Salt
- Baking Soda
- Fruit
- Cocoa
- Syrup
- Butter

Unpacking "Sold" two words: Retail versus Wholesale

Sold: Retail Versus Wholesale

We are in the home stretch here. Details about how product

turned into money would be a huge differentiating factor. It

could be a tie-breaker piece of data with a competing candy-

maker.

- Over-The-Counter
- E-Commerce
- Mail-Order
- Commercial Shipping
- Cash
- Check
- ATM
- Credit
- Accounts Receivable

Sold: Slice-and-Dice the Numbers

Most of us do not think about how our job ties back to the cash.

Even if you are not sure about the numbers or even hate the

numbers they can be estimated. So long as the estimates are done consistently, your numbers could include:

- Gross Sales
- Net Sales
- Net Cost
- Profits by Category
- Per Day Sales
- Per Week Sales
- Per Month Sales
- Per Quarter Sales
- Annual Sales
- Bulk Pricing
- Unit Pricing
- How Many
- Which Kind

Sold: What & Who

Refining what was sold can allow us to re-state the same experience from a different perspective to beef our experience without misleading people. Simple items similar to these would work:

- Packages
- Baskets
- Boxes
- Bags
- Seasonal Sales
- Holiday Sales
- Catering Sales
- Special Occasions
- Weddings
- Graduations

Next Step: Start with a Thought

Notice I did not say start with a sentence? We want to be deliberate and create a "thought" at this point in the process. Technically we have been developing our words, right? Developing our vocabulary so we can focus on our thoughts; our thoughts about our experiences.

It seemed to me people would get hung-up on their resume content in a rush and write the perfect sentence. This sounds like a great idea. And because of attribution or bias, people think they are ready to dive in and write the perfect prose.

But in my estimation people need to slow-down and take a Beat. Pause. Exhale.

Why?

The thought is easier to create than the perfect sentence. The rush to Sentence-Hood has derailed more than a few resume efforts. It has probably undermined people's confidence without them realizing it, too.

The raw or incomplete thought is easier and faster to create. It is more flexible when changing it and creating variations.

That is the goal right now - create a thought.

The Thought-Template

To give this process some structure I instituted a concept we will call the Thought-Template. This is nothing more than a check-list. You can use a spread-sheet, word processor or paper and pen.

By being deliberate with this process we accomplish the following:

- Efficient brainstorming
- Organize content creation
- Offload short-term memory
- Overcome unconscious competence
- Get reacquainted with your expertise

Brainstorming is natural for some people but not others. By using a check-list we can facilitate the creation of more content. Using this check-list will also organize your content which will make it easier to review, refine or outright change it easier than a full-blown sentence.

Offloading short-term memory is one of my pet-projects. People do not realize much of their angst or nervousness is from over-loading their memory. Lists are a cheap solution. Keeping the short-term memory "empty" can calm the nerves and allow the brain room to think.

Unconscious competence is probably the main reason people are unable to explain what they do for a job in a resume. Unconscious competence happens to all of us. It is great for motor-skill related task like driving or playing sports. It comes in real handy at work performing the required tasks. But unconscious competence is the enemy of resume content creation. Forcing yourself to use this check-list will expedite the process in the long run.

How?

It will help you recover or become reacquainted with both the vocabulary of your industry but also with your experiences.

This is key because most of us file away the good-stuff! Think back to your last certificate or award. Did you mount it on high or email blast your network? No. You filed it away – along with the experience which earned you the recognition.

Slowing the process is crucial to uncovering those experiences post-event.

The Thought-Template has Four-Parts:

- Action
- Thing
- Environment
- Quantity

Because there are English phobic people in the world I avoid words like verb, noun, adjectives and adverbs. Plus, there is no really good way to explain how to develop quantity related data for a resume.

"Action"

Action is nothing more than the doing-aspect of the job. Technically these would be verbs and adverbs but do not get tied-up in this grammar-detail. Simply ask yourself "what was the action" or "what was executed."

Write down what comes to mind. This can be a single word or phrase. It does not matter. Do it. With practice you will develop a rhythm with your content development.

"Thing"

The "thing" is nothing more than the "it" being acted upon. If the word noun makes you feel better, great. It can also be the name of a project or the topic of your part of the project.

"Environment"

The "environment" might be thought of as "where" things took place. It is likely another noun or pronoun. Nonetheless, you want to unpack the details here. This means not repeating a previous noun in this thought (another noun even).

"Quantity"

Whatever your experience was it can be quantified. In the "Quantity" section you want to provide numerical data. This will be things represented by inventory totals or percentages of inventory or money related items. It can also be different types of dollar amounts resembling cash balances, revenue estimates or projections, operational expenses, capital expenditures or other costs and or savings you created.

These quantities can be estimates as long as you are consistent in your methodology *and* can explain with confidence if asked about your approach.

The Thought-Template Rules:

There are 4 rules to using the Thought-Template:

- Start each thought with an Action-word
- Use 2 more of the remaining 3 parts
- Do not repeat words within the same thought
- The remaining sequence can be in any order

Rule One – Begin with an Action

Opening with an action is an unbreakable rule. Always start with an action (verb/adverb). It sets the thought up to demonstrate your execution in the experience being presented.

Rule Two - Use at Least 2 of the 3 Remaining Parts

This is rather simple – add 2 more pieces of data to your thought. If you can add all 3, great. But logically, if you add 2 pieces of data, when combined with the verb, you automatically have a complete thought ready for editing.

Rule Three - Do Not Repeat the Same Words

By not repeating the same word (in any solo thought) you will force yourself to develop better content automatically. At a minimum following this rule will force you to become well versed in finding and using synonyms. This will keep your content from appearing redundant or repetitive.

Rule Four – After Verb Use Any Sequence

This rule allows you to re-sequence thing, environment, and quantity allowing you can reconstitute your content from many points of view.

Use Synonyms

You want to extend your content using synonyms. Do this to present the same experience or piece of information from different angles.

This will allow you to create multiple perspectives about your experience. These different perspectives allow you to customize the resume for each submission.

The Magic: Thoughts Become Sentences

Once you have the thought-template filled out creating sentences will be less stressful and far more productive.

Your thought-template might look like this:

Action	Thing	Environment	Quantity
1. Made	Hard candies	retail sale	$200
2. Mixed	Fruit and dark	Christmas	400
3. Processed	Spices	company recipe	60 lb.

Using the first thought our sentence might be:

• *Made hard candies for retail sales totally $200 per week*

This is not a bad example and it is a huge improvement over the original content in Sara's resume.

But – take it step further and review it for vagueness. Check each word and ask what is missing.

There are two-ways to think about what is missing:

• A lack of granularity
• Abstract words

Both of these conditions mean there is a level of vagueness and you want to replace these words with something better.

In this case our vague word is: *candies.*

While the statement is not bad and could be used as is; lets unpack "candies" with our synonym list.

That might net experience statements resembling:

- *Made peppermints for retail sales totaling $200 in sales*
- *Made lollipops for retail sales totaling $200 in sales*
- *Made Christmas confectionaries totaling $200 in retail sales*

Compare these last three sentences to the original below:

- *Made hard candies for retail sales totally $200 per week*

Which would you pick?

Peppermint, lollipop, Christmas confectionaries wording generates a visual image which can also activate an olfactory recollection or kinesthetic memories of handling them in the reader.

In two of the granular statements the dollar amount is ahead of the "retail sales" words. Re-ordering the quantity data with the environment can make content creation less stressful.

And once you understand what the process is forcing you to do; you will find a rhythm and knock out content quickly.

Here we have two examples which may make the case for *not* re-ordering the Thought-Template elements.

- *Made wrapped holiday candies selling $200 dollars' worth*
- *Made Christmas mints selling $200 dollars' in OTC sales*

What about these examples coming up?

- Mixed fruit with dark chocolate for 400 units for Christmas
- Processed over 60 lbs. of raw spices per company recipe

The objective is an expression of experience that is clear and as concise as possible which showcases your expertise.

With more content options generated with the Thought-Template the more options you will have for the resume.

Deconstruct Compound Statements

In this example we have what would be considered a normal experience statement in any other resume book.

But if we consider the power of the word *"and"* on a resume we can develop better content.

Read this compound experience statement:

- Mixed and measured ingredients per company recipe for hard candy selling 500 pounds per week.

This sentence is the type we want to avoid in resumes.

Why?

The reader may not get beyond the *"and."* On a standard resume printed or on screen, the *"and"* can be a bump in the reading-road allowing the eye to move off the content; the eye will typically drop to the next line.

They may want specifics on the words before the *"and."*

But for some readers the *"and,"* telegraphs a lack of specifics about those words ahead of it. Few readers will slog through the "and" hoping for those details. Their focus declines and the eyes move on. Boom. They miss any relevant experience in the remaining text. You fail to capture their attention with *"and"* interrupting their interest on the words before it.

The fix?

Break-up the statement at the *"and"* to develop 2 or more independent experience statements!

Dissecting "Mixed and Measured"

If we split the experience statement at the *"and"* we end up with:

- Mixed
- Measured ingredients per company recipe for hard candy selling 500 pounds per week

We can clean this up by repeating the tail-end of the experience statement giving us these redundant statements:

- Mixed ingredients per company recipe for hard candy selling 500 pounds per week
- Measured ingredients per company recipe for hard candy selling 500 pounds per week

The only difference is the Mixed versus Measured word-choice at the front.

Can you see your experience from at least two perspectives?

Will this force you to modify one or both statements?

This will help you identify multiple ways of presenting the same experience from different angles.

You might end with these experience statements as a result:

- Mixed ingredients for our hard candy base-recipe
- Sold 500 pounds of hard candy per week
- Measured ingredients for sour-hard candies

By having two or more discreet experience statements from re-writing the nearly identical statements; we net more granular content. How does this help? *It allows the recruiter and hiring manager to focus on what they think is important.*

This helps the human speed-read your content. Be that easier to deal with candidate!

It also differentiates your experience from the competition. And, you can delete experience not related to the job at-hand, yielding a very tightly focused resume.

Will This Get Me Hired:

In the end, you have to be your own quality assurance check on your resume content.

In the end – you have to decide if the content you share is worthy of a job offer.

Learn to interrogate your content by asking this question over and over: *Will this get me hired?*

Next you want to review your content for clarity and emotional imprinting on the reader.

Why?

If the experience is not clear or fails to produce an emotion - the reader will be apathetic to your content.

Apathy to your content is why they do not call you back!

Now this is where the marketing clowns rear their ugly heads.

And with no offense to clowns, marketers confused hype for emotion. While hype might sell the cars, food or vacations, when it comes to resumes hype will always backfire.

With resumes, emotion comes from granular content.

Hence it is not enough to think or believe your resume writing will get you hired.

We need an extra level of filtering to check our bias with more questions. It is a great way to break ties between similar content. Ask yourself: Which statement variation is easier to:

- Understand
- Read
- Believe
- Comprehend
- Visualize

Record your reaction for each question for each piece of content being reviewed. This can be a point system which can help take the decision process out of your heart and move into your head.

The experience statement with the most check-marks (highest score) would be a starting point for inclusion in the resume. Boom. Done.

Comparing Compound Content to Discreet Statements

While a bit redundant, I *did not* want to force you to flip back and forth between these examples.

Here is what we are comparing; the compound statement with the "*and*" against discreet experience statements.

First the compound statement from before:

- *Mixed and measured ingredients per company recipe for hard candy selling 500 pounds per week.*

Next the possible single-idea per line experience statements we could create:

- *Mixed ingredients per company recipe for holiday hard candy*
- *Sold 500 pounds of hard candy per week*
- *Measured flavor compounds to form hard candy slurry*

While the first example we can agree is a much more efficient to read. We would also agree no one is going to read this many words across multiple lines in a resume!

Why? No one reads your resume for pleasure or nail-biting suspense.

We want the human to "see" the content they care about (allowing them to find their bias and making it speed-reader friendly) by using a less complex sentence structure. This helps make our content granular, too. It forces us to get serious about our content. Welcome to Grown-Up Town!

For the examples listed; answer this question first:

- ***Will this get me hired?***

You want to feel or hear a resounding "Yes" or "No."

A *no* is an invitation to re-write the content now or later. If you do this with your friends, remember your reaction matters most. It is your experience!

For each *yes*, filter that piece of content by asking the following five questions.

Which version of the experience is easier to:

1. Understand
2. Read
3. Believe
4. Comprehend
5. Visualize

The more "yes" reactions for a piece of content, the more confident you can be about it going in your resume.

More Examples to Review

The first question is always:

- **Will this get me hired?**

For each "no" reaction – move on to the next example. For every "yes" response ask these five-questions.

Which version of the experience is easier to:

1. Understand
2. Read
3. Believe
4. Comprehend
5. Visualize

Here are the before and after examples to experiment with.

- Molded jellybeans and licorice using marble top and roller pin techniques to mold pieces and sold $100 worth of product per day.

- Versus -

- Molded jellybeans using marble top and roller pin technique
- Shaped licorice ties free-hand for customize orders
- Sold $100.00 or more of soft candies per day

Use these questions consistently for all of your resume content and Sara's.

By doing this line-by-line it re-enforces the "know-how" and vocabulary.

On average, about 25 minutes of this mental questioning will produce results you can be confident about.

In summary your questions are always as follows:

1. Will this get me hired? Each "yes" is filtered by asking:
2. Which experience is easier to *Understand*
3. Which experience is easier to *read*
4. Which experience is easier to *believe*
5. Which experience is easier to *comprehend*
6. Which experience is easier to *visualize*

Here are more examples of compound experience statements to review:

- Increased production by 200% during Easter promotion by scheduling vendor product deliveries to coincide with staged mixing methodologies
- Used copper mixing bowls, steam kettles and brass molds to produce 1,000 hard candies weekly

Compare to more granular experience statements like these:

- Increased production by 200% during Easter promotion
- Scheduled vendor deliveries based on staged mixing needs
- Used copper mixing bowls to combine specialty ingredients
- Melted hard candy pieces using steam kettle techniques
- Used brass molds to produce 1,000 hard-candies per week

Estimating Numbers

Naturally, if you have documented numbers for your work experience – use them.

But most people tell me they were not numbers people or they were several levels removed from the numbers information.

The solution is to develop estimates.

The process does not have to be technical or complicated. As long as a) you are not misrepresenting the truth and b) can explain your estimates concisely; your estimates will be considered valid.

In our examples we see the number 500 pounds of something being used per week.

We can extrapolate a yearly number by multiplying five-hundred (pounds of an ingredient) by 52 (for weeks in a year) which will net 26,000 (pounds) a year. In this example we would ask:

- Did we work the year?
- Did we use the product for a year?

If the answer is yes and yes, the annual estimate is a reasonable extrapolation from our original 500-pounds.

We use this estimate to showcase our scale of experience.

This is the sizzle in a resume – a detail that demonstrate scale, is easily understood, appears reasonable based on an estimate which is not complicated to explain. Not the marketing hype language recommended by marketing clowns (no offense to the clowns).

The sizzle is in sharing what we did and numbers sell our experience so much better than hollow hyperbolic language.

If we sold a hundred dollars' worth of product a day, we can estimate how-many days per year this took place and do the math.

It might also be easier to think about this in terms of each week, each month, each quarter initially and then roll-out annual estimates. With annual estimates, we can always divide by the weeks, months and quarters to re-state our numbers.

In our example, Sara might tell us that for 300 days of the year she sold $100 dollars' worth of product over the counter. We multiply 300 (for the days) by 100 (for the dollars) and net $30,000. This would be a reasonable estimate of annual sales. We could also back-track and convert the 300 days into a monthly, weekly and quarterly estimate. Not good with this sort of math? Ask Google "how many weeks is 300 days" and it will tell you 42.8571. Ask Google "how many months is 300 days" and will tell you 9.863. Boom. Use the whole number 42 and 9 and you will not over-estimate when you divide $30K by each number ($3,333 for 9 months and $719 for 42 weeks). This would net more experience statement options:

- Sold $3K+ a month for 9 months of soft-chew candies
- Sold $700+ a week for 42 weeks of jaw-breakers
- Sold $30K in hard candies annually
- Sold $30K in hard candies in 300 days
- Sold $30K in hard candies over a 9-month period
- Sold $30K in hard candies in 42 weeks

Which version you use would depend on what else was already on the resume to avoid redundant sounding or redundant looking content. Being able to discuss the numbers for different slices of time (per day, per week or per month) can make great talking points in the interview, too.

Staying in the Truth

We always want to work with the truth. We never want to bend the truth because what you think is *bending* the truth is likely breaking it to somebody else.

So how do you stay in the truth? Work with facts exclusively. When you develop estimates be able to explain the estimate with confidence because the math is simple and the data-points are real.

The Big Resume Secret to Being Qualified

Sharing common job behaviors in the resume will stop disqualifying questions by hiring managers and recruiters. Read that again. *Sharing common job behaviors in the resume will stop disqualifying questions by hiring managers and recruiters.* Showing common job behaviors in the resume will likely stop the hiring manager from filtering your resume with disqualifying questions.

This is the big resume secret.

Fail to demonstrate common job behaviors, the hiring manager will look for ways to disqualify the candidate. This is why candidates are not called. The vague language of marketing hype cannot create this impression.

Demonstrate what are perceived normal or common behaviors on the resume and people stop looking for flaws.

If we start to think about methods, tools and recipes in the case of our Candy Maker, you would notice how those details *do not* generate disqualifying questions about the candidate's experience.

Technically, it is safer for the recruiter (hiring manager, HR team) to disqualify candidates than it is to take a chance on their implied knowledge, skills or abilities.

On the one hand there is this idea of a "unicorn" candidate. It goes something like this in the mind of a hiring manager and some recruiters: "If we weed-through these less-than great people we will ultimately find *the one* who solves all of our problems."

This hiring trap is easy to fall into because it feels like we are being disciplined and vigilant. The fact of the matter is we are not allowing ourselves to find great people. We are holding out for the unicorn candidate (which does not exist, hence the name).

This phenomenon happens because we have experience with interviews with individuals who had poorly done resumes: they never rehabilitate themselves in the process (even though we know hiring managers and recruiters rarely overcome their own confirmation bias).

Or worse we are jaded.

We are immune to the marketing hype of "successfully delivered" or "responsible for" or "seasoned opened-door mentor." We will not risk an interview with another blow-hard, hyper-positive, dogmatic, potentially a former cheerleader or almost turned-pro athlete selling their lack of experience as a plus for my job opening.

But the truth is this type of language on a resume fails because it is void of any information. It states the obvious.

Of course you were:

- Responsible - it was your job
- Successful - no fool shares failure on a resume
- Of course you turned it around, they were almost there

And so it goes.

The Case for Granular Resume Content

As your word choices become more specific, making the experience statements more granular, a mental shift happens in the reader's mind. They engage not only the content itself, but they engage the candidate as well.

This is what I call "the shift."

To explain the shift, think back to a time you decided to dislike a specific neighbor, co-worker, celebrity or politician. This dislike feels genuine and justified in your heart-of-hearts.

Then, later, maybe a few days or a few years out, you hear or learn or read something new about that person and without explanation your dislike changes instantly to a positive attitude about that person. An epiphany happens based on a feeling empathy or appreciation. You want this to happen with the hiring manager when reading your resume.

Why? They are so use to empty or vague content they can project previous disappoint onto your resume unfairly. This feeling manifests itself in the form of disqualifying the candidate line by line on the resume.

But with granular content, specific information about your experience, the hiring manager will shift from disqualifying the candidate to assessing the candidates' fit.

This idea the candidate *could* do the job creeps into their thinking. This is step-one of granular content; stopping the disqualifying analysis.

Step-two is they readily assume through osmosis or exposure, the right people or technology, that the candidate would perform *well enough*.

This shift in thinking is huge. It breaks the disqualifying question-set. It moves the candidate mentally in their mind to being at least a "maybe" hire if not someone worth an offer.

Think about that! A less qualified candidate can beat a better qualified candidate who used marketing hype which is less detailed by its nature.

People fail to realize the sizzle of their experience comes from presenting it; not talking around it in glowing terms.

Being granular and specific with your content opens opportunities marketing-hype cannot.

Sara Elf New Resumes – Comparing Content

Here is an updated elf resume. There are 2-forms of content. In the initial job experience we have granular statements. In the subsequent jobs we used compound statements. Review for yourself:

[New Elf Resume]

Sara Elf
Candy Maker
saraelfcandymaker@gmail.com
North Pole, AK 99705

Candy Maker Preview
Candy maker with expertise in traditional chocolate and hard-candy recipes using modern equipment and old-school counter-top techniques and tools for holiday and personal celebrations.

Candy Maker Expertise
Counter Tech: Copper bowls, molds, ladles, pins, marble
Mixing Tech: Steam, direct heat, air-blown, air brush
Industrial Tools: Hydraulic spreaders, rollers, press molds

Candy Maker Experience

Candy Master, Inc. February 2000 to Present
Candy Maker Elf Village, NP

- Molded jellybeans using marble top and roller pin technique
- Shaped licorice ties free-hand for customize orders
- Sold $100.00 or more of soft candies per day
- Mixed fruit and dark chocolate for Christmas order
- Processed 60+ lbs. of raw spices following company recipe
- Mixed ingredients for our hard candy base-recipe
- Sold 500 pounds of hard candy per week
- Measured ingredients for sour-hard candies for Halloween
- Increased production by 200% during Easter promotion
- Scheduled vendor deliveries to stagger mixing jobs
- Used copper bowls to combine hard candy ingredients
- Applied steam kettle techniques to mold hard-candies
- Prepared brass molds to produce 1,000 pieces per week

Masters of Candy, LLC March 1995 to May 2000
Candy Maker Elf-in Way, NP

- Molded jellybeans and licorice using marble top and roller pin techniques to mold pieces and sold $100 worth of product per day.
- Used copper mixing bowls, steam kettles and brass molds to produce 1000 hard candy pieces weekly.

Candies R Us January 1881 to May 1995
Candy Maker Clause Town, NP

- Mixed and measured ingredients per company recipe for hard candy selling 500 pounds per week.
- Increased production by 200% during Easter promotion by scheduling vendor product deliveries to coincide with staged mixing methodologies.

[End of New Elf Resume]

Elf Resume Debrief and Review

In putting both forms of content on the same resume the risk is people will copy this format on their resume: Do. Not. Do. It. This presentation was made to make it easier to compare the content styles and avoid artificially padding the book.

Sara Elf Resume Debrief

Top of Resume

Sara Elf
Candy Maker
saraelfcandymaker@gmail.com
(907) 555-1212
North Pole, AK 99705

At the top of the resume *(i.e. not in the header)*; we have Sara's name, job title, phone, email and city, state, zip code; centered and in bold-text

REVIEW: This makes Sara's contact information front and center on the resume. It is not in the header, it is not inside a text-box and it is not part of a table. This makes it easy to copy and paste this information into other emails, one-off reports or spreadsheets the recruiter may have to update.

We added the city, state and zip code information so the recruiter can quickly know where Sara is located. The street address is not necessary on the resume.

CHANGE: We also updated Sara's email address and added a phone number (directory assistance in Alaska). This allows for career branding and it makes her email address easier to recall and if she were real, a phone number is essential.

Expertise Preamble

Candy Maker Preview

Candy maker with expertise in traditional chocolate and hard-candy recipes using modern equipment and old-school counter-top techniques and tools for holiday and personal celebrations.

REVIEW: The expertise-preamble has been referred to by other names on legacy-resumes:

- Marque-Statement / Paragraph
- Opening-Statement / Paragraph
- Focus-Statement / Paragraph

We will call it what it is: the *expertise-preamble*.

The expertise-preamble replaces the "objective" statement for those keeping score against legacy resumes.

The *preamble* can trick the human eye into reading the text instead of skimming it alone.

In this case we started with the job title which is typically an excellent keyword option.

The remaining text uses jargon from the candy business. These words should evoke a mental image (chocolate, hard-candies). The mention of recipes tells the reader this person can follow directions. And the contrast of old-school and modern techniques shows the breadth of experience without favoring one over the other.

Lastly, the end of the paragraph should conjure more imagery (holiday / personal celebrations) without limiting it. This text is agnostic on purpose.

Why?

It allows the reader to image *their* preferred holiday (personally or professionally) be it Christmas, Valentine's, Easter, Halloween or Hanukkah. If the job description mentioned a specific holiday-related opening, aligning your content accordingly would be good branding.

The same agnostic-wording applies to "personal celebrations." The human reader is free to assume and image:

- Birthdays
- Weddings
- Holiday Parties
- Catered Events

CHANGE: We use the word *"expert"* because it is stronger than the word *"experience."* Experience is vague by definition.

Expertise Paragraph

Candy Maker Expertise
Counter Tech: Copper bowls, molds, ladles, pins, marble
Mixing Tech: Steam, direct heat, air-blown, air brush
Industrial Tools: Hydraulic spreaders, rollers, press molds

REVIEW: The expertise paragraph can be labeled anyway which makes sense: Summary, Overview, Preview. Any of these would be acceptable alternatives. We bold "Candy Maker Expertise" to help with the resume layout.

In this case we used "Expertise."

We further brand the content with labels at the start of each experience statement. We bold these words and use a colon to separate them from the content logically for the reader.

This *hack* of using two-labels streamlines the over-all resume layout *and* creates a matrix for controlling the eye as it moves across the text. We do this without using tables or tabs or columns as these word processing features can get jacked-up on the ATS.

The keywords following the in-line-label are highly visual without telegraphing specific vendors, makes or models of the items mentioned.

If the job description mentions equipment by name, model or version – replicate those names where you had the experience.

Resume Experience Section

Candy Maker Experience

Candy Master, Inc.   February 2000 to Present
Candy Maker   Elf Village, NP

- Molded jellybeans using marble top and roller pin technique
- Shaped licorice ties free-hand for customize orders
- Sold $100.00 or more of soft candies per day
- Mixed fruit and dark chocolate for Christmas order
- Processed 60+ lbs. of raw spices following company recipe

REVIEW: The label "Candy Maker Experience" replaces traditional labels and their variants such as these:

- Professional Experience
- Professional Summary
- Career Experience

Using the job-title instead of the words *professional* or *career* improves branding and keyword hit-ratios.

Bolding is applied to the entire label, which is centered.

We also bold company name and job title text along the left-margin to guide the eyes.

We do not want to draw the eye off or away from the left-margin so we do not bold text on the right-margin for date and location. Each experience statement starts with a verb or adverb. We assume these parts of speech are ranked higher by the algorithms which score or rank resume content.

Each statement focuses on a single idea. We also want to keep each experience statement to one-line across (given the margin layouts of the book this cannot always be displayed accurately).

EXERCISE: One last practice... review each experience statement and ask the filtering questions once more:

1. Will this get me hired? If "yes" filter again by asking:
2. Which experience is easier to *Understand*
3. Which experience is easier to *read*
4. Which experience is easier to *believe*
5. Which experience is easier to *comprehend*
6. Which experience is easier to *visualize*

Whether you use tick-marks or total up points in a scoring system, this exercise will give you insights to *your* content.

Reviewing your content this closely will help you select the best you have to offer. It will give you clarity of skill and a confidence about your experience no one else can provide.

Experience Continued – Compound Statements

Masters of Candy, LLC   March 1995 to May 2000
Candy Maker   Elf-in Way, NP

- Molded jellybeans and licorice using marble top and roller pin techniques to mold pieces and sold $100 worth of product per day.
- Used copper mixing bowls, steam kettles and brass molds to produce 1000 hard candy pieces weekly.

Candies R Us   January 1881 to May 1995
Candy Maker   Clause Town, NP
- Mixed and measured ingredients per company recipe for hard candy selling 500 pounds per week.
- Increased production by 200% during Easter promotion by scheduling vendor product deliveries to coincide with staged mixing methodologies.

The remaining experience statements are NOT examples of what to do on your resume. They were included here to make it easier to compare them to the granular examples in the first experience section.

The denser content of a compound experience statement makes them harder to read. Harder to read means slower-reading, less-reading or no-reading by the human.

If the reader does not see something of interest in the first 1 to 3 words, they are likely to stop and move their eyes to the next section; without viewing any of the remaining content.

In contrast, the granular content is easier to skim and by discussing one-key idea per line the reader can find what they care about easier, if not faster.

Putting It All Together

All this reading to understand some simple resume content creation techniques is a little annoying, right?

You already knew this stuff from high school, right?

But it was way back in your medial temporal lobe somewhere and my goal was to fish it out and bring it back to the frontal lobe (brain jokes are not knee slappers, sorry).

My point is you have done this before for others and yourself but maybe not for your resume. Now you have it fresh and ready to go.

Things like word association, list making, finding synonyms to re-discover your profession's vocabulary is not exciting. But, it lays the foundation for being able to rapidly recall your work experience.

Learning to slow down the content creation process artificially with a *thought* first does not feel efficient. But it is the precursor to creating granular content.

We care about granular content because we want the hiring manager to stop filtering your resume with disqualifying questions and mentally move themselves to wanting to hire you instead.

And learning to ask questions about your content like: "Will this experience statement get me hired?" takes time; but it will force you to be genuine with how you represent your resume content. Being able to know which experience statement is easier to understand, read, believe, comprehend or visualize is also necessary to make yourself consciously aware of your resume content and get you off resume auto-pilot.

What do you do if what you have done so far is not enough? What if you are so stuck, no matter how great this little exercise is for *other* people, what do people do who need something more? Something more granular?

Vocabulary Help

Nothing sexy here – all work. But it is work you can knock out in an afternoon! In the end you should have more than enough content to create a resume with exceptional granularity with options to customize the resume for each submission.

For blue-collar to white-collar this is my best technical approach to locking down your resume vocabulary.

Amazon

Be sure to search for books in your profession and read the preview, connect to the authors and read the related reviewer. Many times the book preview and reviewers share inside content of terms and phrases used to describe your job experience.

Cross reference all of the Amazon dot options as well: Amazon.Co.UK, Amazon.FR, Amazon.DE, Amazon.NL, Amazon.Co.JP, Amazon.Com.AU, Amazon.CA, Amazon.IT, Amazon.IN and Amazon.CN to name a few.

Wiki Pages

If you do it for love or money, someone has written about it on a Wiki Page. The search for your needs would be [Job-Title Wiki]; replacing the words Job-Title with your research target and omitting the square brackets.

Some examples which may yield slightly different and useful results might be *"programmer wiki"* against *"JAVA wiki"*; *"business analyst wiki"* in contrast to *"project manager wiki."* Realize some companies have their own "wiki" pages separate from the public domain. This means landing on their page and searching inside of their domain.

Glossaries

Another search is [glossary job-title]; using your job title, the word *glossary* in an online search (without the brackets).

The search *glossary business analysis* generated over 10M results. It is highly unlikely you need more than 1 or 2 glossaries to work from.

There are also business analysis glossaries listed by industry (i.e. Health Care and IT).

There are glossaries used by state-agencies and countries outside of the USA.

Other job titles like project manager, developer and webmaster have similar results. Software architecture, Internet of Things, Accountant and audit have results of less than a million. There are glossaries for admin assistant, receptionist and call center.

There are glossaries for retail, sales, marketing, social media, franchise, HR, benefits and on and on.

By the way, there are only a few hundred-thousand glossary entries for *candy making!*

Another source of glossaries would be certifying and training web sites. Some of these may require membership login, most do not.

Dictionaries

I know, the word *dictionary* sounds boring. They are. I saw your eyes roll from my keyboard.

But like glossaries, nothing beats content from a professional source to create clarity and granularity in your resume. Whether online, or at a local used book-store, professional dictionaries can be a wealth of information for resume content.

Barron's has a Business Dictionary Series for:

- Finance and Investment
- Business and Economics
- Insurance
- Accounting
- Computer and Internet
- Finance and Investment
- Real Estate
- Banking
- International Investment
- Mathematics
- Tax

Other names you might recognize include the people from

McGraw-Hill and Penguin:

- Dictionary of Electrical & Computer Engineering by McGraw-Hill
- Penguin Dictionary of Civil Engineering

Then we have more examples across several disciplines:

- Newton's Telecom Dictionary by Steven Schoen and Gail Saari

- Dictionary of Project Management Terms (Third Edition) by J. LeRoy Ward
- Glossary of Supply Chain Terminology. a Dictionary on Business, Transportation, Warehousing, Manufacturing, Purchasing by Philip Obal
- Official Dictionary of Purchasing and Supply by H.K. Compton and DA Jessop
- Dictionary of Human Resources and Personnel Management: Over 8,000 Terms Clearly Defined (have fun memorizing that bad-boy) by A. Ivanovic and Peter Collin
- The SAGE Dictionary of Qualitative Management Research
- The New Relational Database Dictionary: Terms, Concepts, and Examples by C. J. Date
- Dictionary of Operations by Konrad Becker and Hakim Bey
- A Dictionary of Civil, Water Resources & Environmental Engineering by Harry C. Friebel
- Dictionary of Aeronautical Terms: Over 11,000 Entries by Dale Crane
- Dictionary of Oil, Gas, and Petrochemical Processing by Alireza Bahadori and Chikezie Nwaoha
- Environmental Engineering Dictionary by C. C. Lee Ph.D.
- Dictionary of Computer Science and Engineering by G, Mr. HemaKumar and P, Dr. Punitha
- Dictionary of Architecture and Construction Feb 18, 2000 by Cyril M. Harris

Oxford Quick Reference has a few options available as well:

- A Dictionary of Mechanical Engineering (Oxford Quick Reference) by Tony Atkins and Marcel Escudier
- A Dictionary of Chemical Engineering (Oxford Quick Reference) by Carl Schaschke

You get the idea – there is a treasure trove of help available if you will only take the time and look.

Lexicon

Want to *know* (not guess) the historical origin, contextual meaning and evolution and usage of a specific *word* or *phrase*; open a lexicon.

A lexicon is a great way to become completely intimate with the language of your profession. A lexicon (in most cases) explains the vocabulary of an industry or topic and how it has changed over time and why. Having this sort of deep knowledge is already in you, technically. Pulling it out of your subconscious can take a lot of mental effort. A lexicon can facilitate that exchange with your synaptic storage (memory, wink)

Think of it this way, a lexicon is the vocabulary of a person, language, or branch of knowledge (i.e. your job title).

The search is the same as the others [lexicon job-title]; minus the brackets and an actual job-title replacing the words *job-title*.

Resume Help

Fiverr.Com

If you have heard my lecture or read my first-book you know I have a bias against using resume writers for developing your resume-content.

With that said, I am not opposed to obtaining *writing help*! Never go it alone; instead, spend your money prudently to assess and test the quality of the help you are buying in an incremental fashion!

With the internet, you have several options for help for very little money if you know where to look.

My experience has been with Fiverr.Com.

You can Google competitors to find other resources, like Upwork or Freelancer. For the record, as of this writing, I am not affiliated in any fashion with Fiverr, Upwork or Freelancer. Honestly, I grudgingly tried Fiverr sellers and, looking back, wish I had spent more money with them! My first book was edited by three different professionals who were all nice people, all qualified to help me and all highly recommended. But the initial spend was crazy money (I could have bought a Life Fitness® Functional Trainer crazy-money). And in the end, I still did not have a properly edited book. Fiverr was my salvation moving forward.

What is Fiverr?

Fiverr is a global online marketplace offering services. Their price point begins at $5 per job. Naturally, service providers upsell items or suggest premium gig offers for more money. You do not have to buy these extras unless you need them. Aside premium service costs, for literally five bucks you can hire a writing professional. My recommendation is search for an "editor non-fiction."

As of this writing, for five bucks, you can hire most editors to review between 1,800 to 2,200 words. This means you are paying pennies per word to have professional help!

To make this painless, I recommend using a single word processing document, include your cover letter, your resume and thank you card blurbs.

Given the size of most resumes, you could include 2 to 3 versions of the resume or add your LinkedIn profile text and still be under the word-limit of most $5 gigs.

Instruct the editor to: "check for typos, word-choice, verb-agreement and hyperbolic language."

This approach allows you to harness the power of a fresh set of professional and dispassionate eyes on your resume content to avoid common problems for little money.

If you are not happy with the outcome, ask for a do-over. If you are not happy with the do-over, ask for a refund. Fiverr makes customer satisfaction their primary focus.

My Fiverr Experience

Initially, I sourced talent out of Fiverr as a recruiter. Great tool for finding people with a select expertise. Once the books were written, I hired several people through Fiverr to complete numerous projects for me.

This included people like the seller "BookConvert." She/he/they (not sure) did my Kindle conversions. They take your Word document and fix it as a Kindle file. You upload to https://kdp.amazon.com/, answer a few questions and you are a published author.

All in, I spent approximately $60 bucks across two versions of the book. Yes, I was a little disappointed that I could *not* have my 159-page file re-formatted, coded, resized for five bucks.

But in this area, it appears to be common practice to pay for the appointment or initial consult to review what is necessary for success.

What did it save me at a $60 dollars spend? Around $440.00 over a "friend" who offered to help. The friend wanted $500 dollars.

There was the seller "Nickih" who is a straight-up editor on a side project for published articles. She offered her premium one-day turn around service for another $10, which I needed. All in, I spent a whopping $15 after the second-round. What did it save me? My original editors charged me from $100 to $125 dollars per hour! Net savings would easily be around $85.00. My new friends "Daswifty", "Aamato", and "Heinseberg" drove my total spend upwards of $50 bucks for a set of 3D-book graphics for the web-page collectively.

It was an artificial deadline I imposed on myself. I needed something for the *Resume Psychology* (RP) web site. This drove me to use 3 people simultaneously. Given my results, it is the best way to go if you need multiple perspectives. My initial amount spent was a mere $15.00. Again, the more complex work, you will pay $5 for the consultation. In the case of my 3D-book graphics, my specification was simple: no shadow, transparency, angle, tones, colors and so on were discussed in great detail.

Given the time differences, I was getting fresh content every hour throughout the night. It was awesome *not* having to wait (or spend too much money). I could test each version against different colors and font sizes.

Each vendor taught me something different about 3D cover graphics, too. What did it save me? Time. Lots of time. Typical turnaround by local vendors was anywhere from a 3-weeks or more. Price? I had a quote from one vendor of $200 per 3D cover option with 2-revisions. Today, there are five variations of my 3D cover PNG file. I would have had to spend $1,000. Conservatively, I saved $150.00, but if you consider I have six variations of my 3D book cover, I probably really saved close to a grand.

Bad-Service on Fiverr

What about disagreements with vendors? I had a few fails, actually. Working with vendors is not all peaches and cream, right? But with Fiverr it can be pretty close. Fiverr has taken much of the risk out of hiring talent.

But... there was the vendor who did not speak (read?) *enough* English to understand what I wanted. He tried. We tried. He/she/they (?) eventually offered to mutually cancel the gig. I pushed a button to agree, and my refund was back in my account in seconds with no questions.

There was also the vendor who wanted to up-sell me to a few hundred bucks more in services. I offered to mutually cancel, and they accepted with no questions. Boom - refund was back in my account with no fuss.

Then, there was the time I heard nothing from the vendor. In my rush to multi-task a few things, this one project fell off *my radar*. The vendor never replied. I never followed up.

Fiverr has a time clock on gigs. Exceed their time limit stipulated by the clock, Fiverr cancels the gig. Boom – the refund went back in my account.

Picking a vendor on Fiverr

Follow the stars. More stars – more better (yes Word wanted to correct more better but I ignored it on purpose).

The Fiverr customer community is vocal and loud, which is probably why mutually agreed upon cancellations are easily obtained.

Hopefully, this information can help you find help for your resume without breaking the bank.

Thank You!

You done?

Thank you for reading. I am grateful for your support.

My goal was to teach an approach to creating consistent resume content with confidence in *your outcomes*.

If nothing else, use the exercise questions to review your content and consider finding inexpensive help online to push yourself along in the writing process.

Kindest regards,

Dirk Spencer

Author, Resume Psychology, The Candy Maker Resume, & Interview Psychology; Available on Amazon.Com

Amazon World-Wide: Amazon.Co.UK - Amazon.FR - Amazon.DE - Amazon.CA - Amazon.IT - Amazon.ES

Author page: www.Amazon.Com/Author/DirkSpencer

Connect to me at: https://www.linkedin.com/in/dirkindallas

Book printer: https://www.createspace.com/5714917

My blog - http://resumepsychology.blogspot.com/

Online presentations: http://www.slideshare.net/dirkspencer

My Twitter is @DirkInDallas

Dirk Spencer BIO

Dirk Spencer is a former government analyst, turned corporate recruiter and author of *Resume Psychology Resume Hacks & Traps Revealed - Beat the Machine. Be Seen. Get Hired!* A fact-based, science-focused approach to modern resumes.

Dirk shares his technical and process insights to help people hack their resumes to be more effective when applying to job openings.

Mr. Spencer has presented *Resume Psychology* to several professional associations from Dallas to Denver, including: Pikes Peak Recruiter Network, Inter-City Personnel Associates, Executive Search Owners Association, American Society for Quality Conferences, National Investor Relations Institute, International Institute of Business Analysis, Intuit Women's Network, Texas Workforce Commission and Dallas Fort Worth Texas Recruiters Network (DFWTRN).

He has also volunteered his time to present *Resume Psychology* to Career Transition Groups such as: Career Jump Start FUMC Richardson, Carrollton Career Focus Group, Carrollton City Job Hunt 101, Crossroads Bible Church Career Transition, Fort Worth Career Search Network, FWCSN Resume Boot Camp Job Angels Network, MacArthur Blvd Baptist Church, Preston Trail Job Network, McKinney Workforce Networking, Southlake Focus Group.

Dirk has also presented *Resume Psychology* to diverse ecumenical groups as well: Jewish Family Service (JFS), Career Counseling Group of DFW Islamic Association of North Texas (IANT), Career Counseling Group of DFW Islamic Center of Irving (ICI), McKinney Trinity Presbyterian Church Career Transition Network, St. Philip's Episcopal of Frisco Job Ministry, St. Andrew UMC Sales Group, St. Jude Career Alliance a Chapter of the Catholic Career Development Community.

In his off-time the author does amateur nature photography, makes Christmas decorations year-round, folds origami-crafts and designs DIY exercise equipment.

Acknowledgments: Blane and Larry

Guys, the Candy Maker lecture let alone *The Candy Maker Resume*, would not have happened without your kind badgering over the years.

I appreciate you both for your unwavering support of the *Resume Psychology* (RP) material and being tolerant of my refractory response on the topic of providing a how-to example for the masses.

God bless you both!

Made in the USA
San Bernardino, CA
05 November 2018